The Stellar Way
Discovering the Star Within

By

Tina Donovan MSEd, LPCC

Illustrated By

James Koenig

The Stellar Way: Discovering the Star Within

Author, Tina Donovan

Illustrator, James Koenig

Editor, Sarah Kolb-Williams

Star Bright Adventures, LLC

330 N. Main Street

Suite 104

Centerville, OH 45459

www.discoverytales.org

www.facebook.com/discoverytales

"The Stellar Way is an exceptional resource that has evolved through years of experience. The characters are created with specific therapeutic messages and with much love by Tina Donovan. A brilliant way to address and transform challenging behavior while increasing emotional IQ and social competency skills. Its creative, robust design makes it an effective resource for professional counselors in any environment. This book is a must-have for every counselor's practice."

-Dr. Patrice Moulton, psychologist, licensed professional counselor, marriage and family therapist, addiction therapist, author, Fulbright specialist

———

In today's culture, so much emphasis is put on fame and fortune, and at times it can seem like very little is put on integrity and character. Unfortunately, a lot of children have picked up the idea that being great doesn't have to include a great attitude. Enter Sparky, a much-needed mascot for emotional development, and The Stellar Way, a fantastic, wonder-filled story that will inspire children to overcome personal challenges and shine brightly.

"A delightfully fun, creative, and adventurous tale, The Stellar Way is a unique way to teach children valuable lessons for emotional growth and development. Beautifully illustrated by James Koenig, The Stellar Way is enchanting, engaging, and beautifully written. Tina Donovan sets out to create a character that will fulfill a void seriously lacking in children's literature—and nails it. Not only can children be entertained and delighted by the story, they can also be challenged and guided in how to better handle their developing emotions and feelings. The Stellar Way is a win-win for parents, children, and educators.

We are pleased to award The Stellar Way the Dove Seal of Approval for All Ages."

- The Dove Foundation

"As an educator, I'm seeing an alarming increase in behavioral issues from children who don't know how to take responsibility for their own feelings and reactions to anger. This desperately needed intervention for students is presented in a unique way by Tina Donovan."

-Laura Bentley, certified teacher, 21 years

———

"The Stellar Way allowed dialogue with three teenage clients, giving me information I had not gotten previously. I found it to be an excellent tool and I highly recommend it!"

-Becky Bergert, LPC, owner of New Dawn Counseling Center

———

"The Stellar Way is a wonderfully written book that will resonate with children of all ages. The artwork is visually striking and the story's message is beneficial. Students, teachers, counselors, and parents will use this book again and again!"

-Sandra Byrd Lawson, author of chapter books Mila Denton's Worst Week Ever! and Mila Denton Is an April Fool!

———

"Tina Donovan's The Stellar Way is a fantastic resource for those who wish to help the children in their lives let go of anger and find their inner star."

-Dorri Hegyi, children's librarian

"Anger and frustration can be very difficult emotions for children to understand and manage. Tina Donovan's The Stellar Way is a powerful book that provides children with the coping skills that allow them to verbalize their thoughts and feelings, learn new ways to cope with problems they face, and understand that having a winning attitude can help through difficult situations."

-Di Riseborough, registered psychotherapist, author of Forgiveness: How to Let Go When It Still Hurts (featured on the Oprah Winfrey Network)

———

"As a speaker and author who encourages others to be the 'star' of their own lives, I highly recommend this book with a similar message to children."

-Curtis Zimmerman, best-selling author of Life at Performance Level

Acknowledgments – Counting My Lucky Stars!

My heartfelt gratitude to all those who have been part of my journey. I am truly grateful for ALL of my family, friends, and colleagues who have helped me along the way, with special acknowledgments to the members of my creative team who embody and exemplify the spirit of The Stellar Way:

James Koenig, my illustrator, for being my superhero and bringing my dream to life. Your phenomenal work combined with your gentle spirit and attention to detail has been a godsend!

Tiger Kandel and Heather Schloss, puppet designers and puppet makers—a dynamic duo, with backgrounds in art therapy and design—for making a seemingly impossible mission possible with their sheer determination, passion, and talents.

Sarah Kolb-Williams, my editor extraordinaire, for her knowledge, invaluable suggestions, enthusiasm, and willingness to go above and beyond to deliver accurate, timely feedback.

and:

Gale Gyure, my writing coach, who met with me weekly for an entire year as I wrote and rewrote The Stellar Way. Gayle graciously shared her home, time, and expertise to gently guide and encourage me.

Regina Frank, Imocaryl Livingston, Brenda Ludwig, Repali Rege, and Watt Smith, my colleagues and friends with diverse backgrounds, whose initial resounding support of The Stellar Way gave me hope of its universal appeal.

Rebekkah Brewer-Klontz, my confidant and friend, who devoted countless hours to bringing The Stellar Way to life. My eternal gratitude for your love and loyal support!

Flora Igah, Margaret Lawson, Renee Price, Pam Miller-Girton, Judy Wilson, and the late Rev. Bill Youngkin, my spiritual mentors, teachers, and counselors for being my guiding lights and showing me the way.

Sylvia Bertke (and children), Don and Lynn Bourne, Mike and Cindy Bourne, Rita Chasteen, Robin Galloway, Sarah Keating, Dick and Meridean Maas, and Diane Scott, my family and friends whose advice, suggestions, and feedback were essential in the development of the characters and whose love and support I cherish.

David's United Church of Christ congregation, Fairmont West High School classmates, and the Cabin Crew, who have blessed me with irreplaceable, lifelong friendships and whose individual and collective company feels like family.

Target Corporation for its generosity in funding the creation of the website.

This book is dedicated with love to:

My husband Tom, my "rock," for believing in me and helping me every step along the way and whose love and support made this possible.

And my mom, who gives me signs that she's very much alive and continues to look after us. It seems only appropriate that we celebrate your eighty-fifth birthday with the book launch. Happy birthday, Mom!

- Tina Donovan -

To my future children, may you always shine brightly in this world.

- James Koenig -

Kelly stormed into her room, threw herself down on her bed, and sobbed, "I hate my miserable, rotten life. I want a new life. This one stinks!"

She took off her dance shoes and continued to rant and rave. "This isn't fair! I should have won. Martha won because she's rich and popular. Susan won because she's cute. I would have won too if I spent as many hours in front of the mirror as she does. She might as well wear mirrors for as often as she looks at herself. Besides, she doesn't have to deal with curly red hair or a zillion freckles like I do," Kelly lamented. "This just stinks!"

Losing the dance competition had catapulted Kelly into a rotten mood, a really big rotten mood. Kelly's anger was like a fiery volcano. Dark black puffs were oozing out of her like a hissing, swirling smokestack sending warning signals to STAY AWAY!

"Martha and Susan were the stars today," Kelly wailed. "I want to be a star. I'd give anything to be a star. I know," she said as she sat up. "I've got a great idea: I'll wish upon a star! 'Star light, star bright, the first star I see tonight. I wish I may, I wish I might have the wish I wish tonight.'"

Kelly clamped her eyes shut, and as if on demand, her cheeks swelled, her nose wrinkled, and her teeth clenched as she focused on her wish. "I wish I was a star. I wish I didn't have this miserable, rotten life. I want a new life, and I want to be a star in it!"

SWOOSH! A whirl of light streaked through the window.

"What on earth, who . . . what are you?" Kelly gasped.

"My name is Sparky. I am answering your wish."

"Oh, brother—this is just my luck. I didn't wish for a star, I wished to be a star."

"My little one, only you can accomplish that," Sparky began. "I can't zap you into a star, but I can teach you how to become one."

"I guess that is better than nothing," Kelly said reluctantly. "What do I do? Let's get started."

"The good news is—you already are a star," Sparky said.

"I am?" Kelly questioned. "I don't feel like a star."

"That's because your anger is like a gigantic chip on your shoulder. It's blocking your light and keeping you from shining like a star," Sparky replied. "If you want to be a star, you need to shine like you are one. I'll show you."

With the speed of light, Sparky grabbed Kelly's hand and they streaked through the sky. In a flash, they stood on a wispy cloud in front of the Galaxy All-Star Camp. The majestic camp stretched for miles. It had eight long, winding corridors that made it look like an octopus with watermelon-shaped feet snapped to its coiled legs.

Kelly's mouth dropped and her eyes opened wide.

"This place is awesome," Kelly exclaimed.

"Well, after all," Sparky said wryly, "this is the place for the stars!"

"As your tour guide and trainer, I believe our first stop is registration. Complete this form and make sure you fill in all the blanks," Sparky directed.

Eagerly, Kelly grabbed the form and glanced at the different sections. Thoughts of becoming a star darted and danced in her mind, taking center stage, holding Kelly's attention.

Her surroundings seemed to shrink as she focused intently on the directions.

COUNT YOUR "LUCKY STARS"

"Kelly, please follow along with me as I read the directions. Anger takes away from our own ability to shine. To be a star, one must shine in both good and bad circumstances. On the form below, write down your blessings—or "lucky stars," as they are sometimes called," Sparky explained.

"That sure will be a short list," Kelly said, thinking aloud.

"In the next section, write down all the things that you don't like about your life and/or things in your life that you would like to change," Sparky directed.

"That sure will be a long list," Kelly said under her breath.

Kelly's pen seemed to have a life of its own as she wrote her lists.

Take Inventory

COUNT YOUR LUCKY STARS - Blessings

Count your blessings!

- My brother sometimes lets me play with him and his friends.

- I like spending time with my relatives in Iowa.

- Sometimes I stay the night at my friend's house.

- I have many good friends.

- I like going to camp.

- My dog doesn't talk back to me.

- I love to dance.

COUNT YOUR CHIPS - The Things That Block Your "Light"

Things I do not like
Things I want to change:

- I hate losing and I want to win a dance competition.
- My dog likes my brother better than me.
- My brother doesn't study at all and he gets A's. I study for hours and get C's.
- I have to share my bedroom with my baby sister.
- My friends all have bigger houses than me.
- I didn't make the cheerleading squad.
- I am not as smart as other kids.
- I am not in the popular crowd.
- My brother gets to stay up later at night.
- My brother gets to go to parties, but my parents say that I am not old enough.
- My little sister gets all the attention.

Sparky checked on Kelly just as her pen seemed to pause for a break. Kelly placed the pen on the desk and assured Sparky that she was done with her lists.

THE MAGNIFICENT MAGNITUDE METER

The Magnificent Magnitude Meter was the next stop on their tour. The scale seemed to stand at attention as Kelly and Sparky approached its golden structure.

"What is this contraption?" Kelly questioned.

"The meter measures the amount of light a star shines. Some stars are brighter, and some are fainter. The meter determines whether you have enough light power to shine like a star. Remember, if you are going to be a star, you need to shine like you are one!" Sparky said with authority.

"Let me try," Kelly said as she grabbed the lever. Then she pulled it down, ever so slowly, and anxiously awaited the results.

The meter's needle seemed to teeter out of its totter before tilting toward the DANGEROUSLY LOW LIGHT POWER setting.

"Oh, my," Kelly gasped. "What . . . what does this mean?"

"You see, Kelly, right now you are carrying so much anger that you are blocking all of your light. You are focusing on what is bad with your life rather than focusing on what is good by counting your blessings, or as some like to say, by 'counting your lucky stars.'"

"It's easy to count your blessings when you have a ton of blessings to count. It's easy to 'count your lucky stars' when you are lucky, but I don't feel lucky," Kelly said defensively under her breath.

"Being a star means that you need to let go of your anger, stop comparing how you stack up against others, and start focusing on what you do have," Sparky said.

"Start focusing on what I do have," Kelly repeated slowly, trying to digest Sparky's words, half choking on them as she realized the challenge ahead.

"Being a star means everything that we do, think, feel, and believe impacts our starability!" Sparky continued.

Starability, Kelly thought. She liked how it sounded and began to soften. "How long does it take to let go of our chips and be a star?" she asked.

"That depends on you, Kelly. I've known some who just naturally shine like a star. Others allow their anger to block their ability to shine. Some use their anger to make their lives better. And some go through their entire lives holding on to their anger so tightly that it ends up being their entire life—one angry, miserable life. I'll show you," Sparky said as he opened the doors to the Launching Pad and directed Kelly to look at the former stars.

"Whoah! Do I look like that . . . like them?" Kelly exclaimed in dismay over their appearance.

Sparky nodded his head in agreement.

"Wow! I had no idea I looked like that! That's ugly—really ugly!" Kelly said, absorbing the magnitude of her anger.

"As I just mentioned, Kelly, some of these stars use this area as motivation to increase their starability and can be launched as a shooting star in a very brief time. Others cling to their anger and have been here for most of their lives."

"Why don't they just let go of their chips?" Kelly inquired.

"Letting go would mean they would need to be responsible for their own feelings, and some believe it is easier to blame others. Anger seems to be their primary way of operating. So they continue with their comfortable habits and patterns— even if letting go would be better for them. Does this make sense?" Sparky questioned.

"I think so," Kelly said, elaborating. "It's kind of like reaching the age of letting go of your teddy bear—you don't really want to do it, but you risk being teased if you don't."

"Exactly!" Sparky exclaimed.

STAR OVERLOOK

"The tenth floor will be our last stop on the tour—the Star Overlook," Sparky explained.

"Oh, my . . ." Kelly gasped in astonishment as they stood on the cloud overlooking thousands of stars. The stars looked like randomly sprinkled diamonds in the sky. Some formed various shapes: a dolphin, a peacock, and twin bears. The most famous constellations, the Big Dipper and the Little Dipper, seemed to demand special attention.

"Kelly, the choice is yours to make," Sparky said. "You can shine like a star or not . . . it is that simple."

"That's easy," Kelly replied. "I want to be a star—I want to shine like those stars—I want to win the next dance contest!"

"Tell you what: why don't you take off that big chip on your shoulder and leave it right here? After school for the next week or so, I'll help you practice your dancing," Sparky assured her.

"Great! You have a deal!" Kelly said enthusiastically.

Each night after school, they practiced, practiced, and practiced some more. They danced and they danced.

They danced until the two slid out of the step,

the jitter twisted out of the bug,

and the fox dropped out of the trot.

Kelly's anger seemed to melt away as her confidence grew with each practiced step.

On the day of the big dancing competition, Sparky brought Kelly back to the Magnificent Magnitude Meter. "Let's see how you are doing, Kelly. Step up onto the meter and let's see if you are shining like a star," Sparky directed. "Much better!" he exclaimed as the needle tilted toward SHINING LIKE A STAR.

Like butterflies, anticipation circled in Kelly's stomach as she waited to go onstage that evening. Her legs felt heavy and stiff, and her feet tingled as she took center stage, but quickly her tightness disappeared as she performed each step with ease and grace.

Kelly radiated from the top of her head to the tips of her toes. She felt like a star. Kelly finished her last step and beamed— beamed proudly because she did great! She just knew she was going to win.

Kelly flapped her hands, pacing a bit as she nervously waited for the winners to be announced.

"Tonight's first-place award goes to . . . Celina Spencer! Our second-place award goes to . . . Samantha Scott! And the third-place award goes to . . . Sarah Martin!"

Kelly's heart sank. The lump in her throat seemed to expand as she tried to catch her breath. "I can't believe this," Kelly said under her breath. She felt the chip on her shoulder growing, dimming her light.

Suddenly, like a parrot repeating its lines, Kelly heard Sparky's echoing message: "If you want to be a star, you need to shine like you are one . . . if you want to be a star, you need to shine like you are one."

Kelly's light began to shine as she decided to remove the chip from her shoulder. Then, just as she stood back up, Kelly heard, "And tonight's special spirit award goes to . . . Kelly Bourne!"

A burst of applause sounded as Kelly practically floated to receive the special spirit award. Kelly beamed with pride.

And so did Sparky.

About The Author

The unwavering commitment of Tina Donovan, MSEd, LPCC, to bring her divinely inspired story The Stellar Way to life has spanned seventeen years, as she has both personally and professionally experienced the need for anger management within our schools and communities. Tina's interest in anger began during her eight-and-a-half-year involvement with the juvenile court system. It seemed that every child who walked into that court had a chip on their shoulder. While this chip manifested in different ways, she noticed one element common to all cases: anger. Tina developed a strong desire to proactively help children with their anger, which led her to pursue and complete her master's degree. She then developed a researched-based, research-tested curriculum that uses concrete tools and activities to help children process and deal with their anger—with the help of a very special superhero, Sparky.

Tina's research was recognized by the Miami Valley Counseling Association, and she was awarded the Wray Rieger Scholarship Memorial Award for her potential to make the most impact in the counseling field. Tina has her own private practice in Centerville, Ohio and specializes in treating children with emotional and behavioral issues.

About The Illustrator

James Koenig is an illustrator who resides in Arizona. He lives with his wife, Corissa, and dog, Bailey.

James started drawing almost as soon as he was born. It was always a passion of his and eventually made it a career when he grew up. Whether he has truly grown up is still up for debate. James has illustrated for over 40 books over his career so far. Along with books, he has also developed characters and artwork for countless products, toys, games, and more.

You can see more of his work at his website: www.freelancefridge.com.

69388920R00031

Made in the USA
Middletown, DE
24 September 2019